P
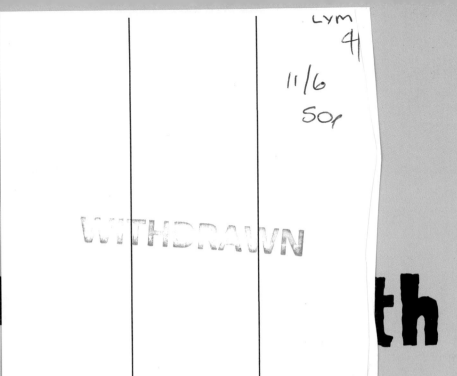
th

Written by Jaclyn Crupi
Illustrated by Patrizia Donaera
Cartoon illustrations by Jane Porter

Consultant: Dr Kim Dennis-Bryan
Educational consultant: Geraldine Taylor

A catalogue record for this book is available from the British Library

Published by Ladybird Books Ltd
80 Strand, London, WC2R 0RL
A Penguin Company

001
© LADYBIRD BOOKS LTD MMXIV
LADYBIRD and the device of a Ladybird are trademarks of Ladybird Books Ltd

ISBN: 978-0-71819-356-0

Printed in China

Contents

Fabulous Facts

Monthly moves

The Moon is a rock that orbits the Earth. It takes about twenty eight days to complete one orbit of the Earth.

Moon

Earth

In a spin

The Earth spins slowly on its axis. This is an imaginary line running through the planet from the top to the bottom.

Night and day

At any one time, half of Earth faces towards the Sun and the other half faces away from it. This changes as the Earth spins around. When it is night in the United Kingdom, it is morning in Australia!

Goodnight!

Good morning!

Wow!

The centre of Earth is called the core. It is a ball of metal that is as hot as the surface of the Sun!

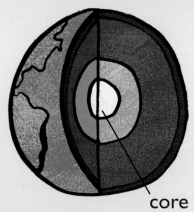

core

Super stars

The stars you can see at night are actually suns far, far away in other solar systems.

What is planet Earth?

Earth is the name of the planet that we live on. It is one of eight planets in our solar system. The Sun is at the centre of our solar system and all planets move around the Sun. Earth is the only planet in the solar system where people live.

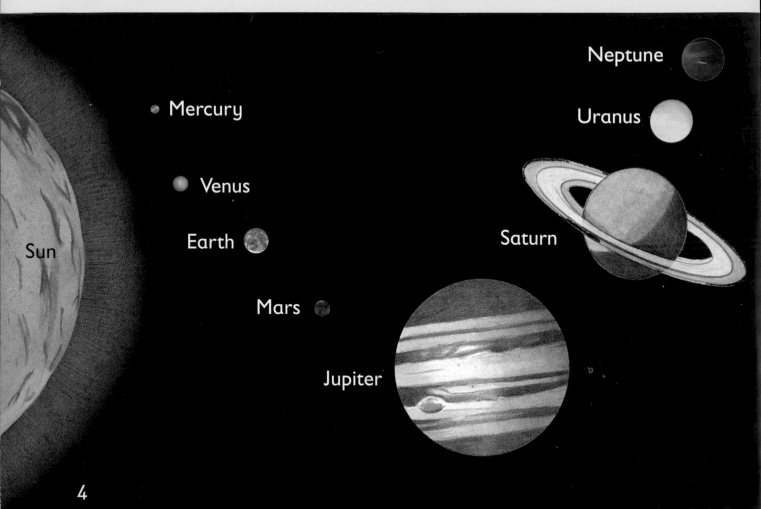

Sun

Mercury

Venus

Earth

Mars

Jupiter

Saturn

Uranus

Neptune

Around the world

Most of Earth's surface is covered in water, which is made up of five oceans. The land is divided into seven continents. A continent is a large area of land and can include many different countries.

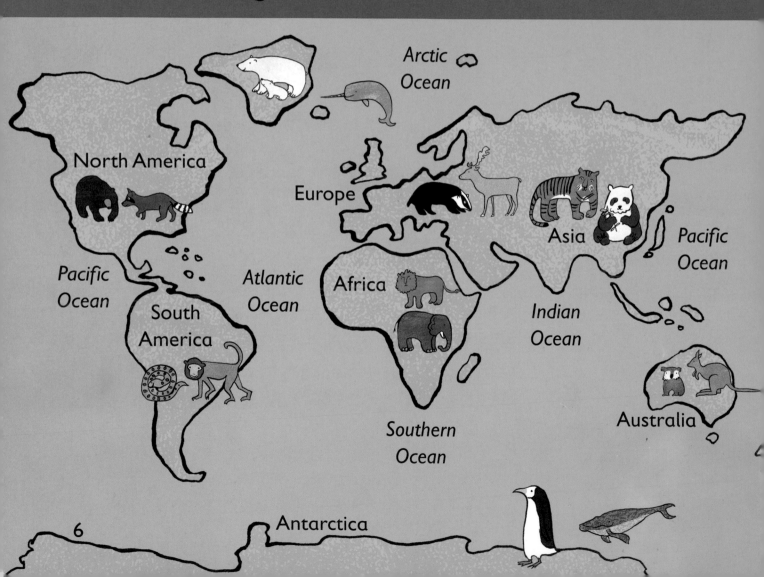

Arctic Ocean

North America

Europe

Asia

Pacific Ocean

Pacific Ocean

Atlantic Ocean

Africa

Indian Ocean

South America

Australia

Southern Ocean

Antarctica

Fabulous Facts

One world

More than 300 million years ago, most of the land on Earth was joined together as one huge continent. Scientists call this continent Pangaea.

River to sea

Water runs off the land into streams. These streams get bigger until they form rivers that eventually lead to seas and oceans.

Get up and go!

About 150 years ago, the fastest sailing ship took around seventy days to sail from the UK to Australia. Today, the same journey by aeroplane takes just one day.

Wow!

Earth is home to an incredible 9 million species of living things.

Squawk!

Volcanoes and earthquakes

The outside of the Earth, called the crust, is made of pieces of rock called tectonic plates. These plates move very slowly on top of red-hot runny rock called magma. These movements can cause volcanoes and earthquakes.

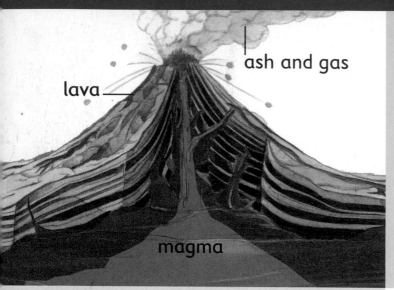

ash and gas

lava

magma

Violent volcanoes

A volcano is an opening in the Earth's crust that forms above the point where two tectonic plates meet. Sometimes, magma bursts up through the volcano. Magma is called lava when it is above the ground.

Dangerous ground

An earthquake is a sudden shaking of the ground. It happens when tectonic plates slide past one another and push and pull in different directions. Sometimes, the Earth's surface will crack.

Fabulous Facts

Not again!

Most earthquakes last less than one minute. After an earthquake, there are often lots of smaller earthquakes called aftershocks.

Pop-up island

Volcanoes can erupt under the sea. When the lava cools and turns into rock, it can sometimes build up to make an island.

Earthquake power

Scientists measure earthquake strength using the Richter scale. The most powerful earthquake happened in Chile in 1960. It measured 9.5 on the Richter scale.

That's big!

Monster waves

Earthquakes and volcanoes at sea can cause giant waves called tsunamis (soo-nah-mees). They are so powerful that they can destroy everything in their path when they hit the land.

Wow!

Earthquakes can make buildings shake and some even fall down. Buildings like the Transamerica Pyramid in San Francisco, USA, where earthquakes happen often, are designed not to collapse in an earthquake.

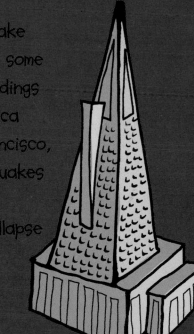

What is weather?

Weather is all around us, all the time. When the air, sunshine and water mix together in different ways, we get different types of weather.

Light flashes

Lightning is made when drops of water and ice rub together in clouds and make electricity. Fork lightning is lightning that hits the ground.

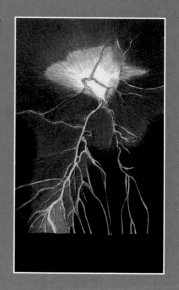

Rainbows

You sometimes see a rainbow when there is sunshine soon after rain. The colours of a rainbow always appear in the same order — red, orange, yellow, green, blue, indigo and violet.

Rain, rain go away...

Rain happens when drops of water fall from clouds in the sky.

Forecasting

Weather forecasters study the weather. They tell us what the weather will probably be like over the next few days.

Fabulous Facts

Starry snowflakes

Snowflakes have six points and are very beautiful when seen close up. Each snowflake has a different shape.

Floods and droughts

Too much rain can cause floods, but if there is no rain over a long period of time, crops cannot grow. This is called a drought.

Help!

Wicked twisters

Tornadoes are made up of swirling winds as fast as 500 kilometres per hour. They can destroy everything in their path.

Weather power

We can use wind and sunshine to make electricity. Solar panels use energy from the Sun. Large wind turbines turn wind power into electricity.

Wow!

Hailstones are lumps of ice that fall from the sky. They are usually smaller than peas, but the largest hailstone ever measured 43 centimetres around its middle – about the size of a pet cat!

That was close!

11

What are rainforests?

Rainforests are forests that have tall trees and are both hot and wet. The Amazon, one of the world's longest rivers, flows through a rainforest in South America. It is home to many thousands of different animals and plants.

red howler monkey

hummingbird

jaguar

green anaconda

caiman

Fabulous Facts

No room for rain

The top of a rainforest is called the canopy. It is so tightly packed together that it can take ten minutes for rain to pass through it to the ground.

Rainforest people

For many thousands of years, people have lived in rainforests, hunting animals and collecting plants. Today, large areas of rainforest have been cleared for farmland and timber. This has forced some people to move.

Trees of life

Rainforests are full of plants and trees that put oxygen back into the air. This is very important to people because we need oxygen to breathe.

Wow!

The largest flower in the world is Rafflesia arnoldii. At about 1 metre wide, it would fill your bath. It also has a really horrible smell – a bit like rotting meat!

Yuck!

What are deserts?

Deserts are the driest places in the world. They are mostly very hot during the day and cool at night, but some can even be cold during the day. Only a few animals are able to survive in the burning heat, and many only come out at night.

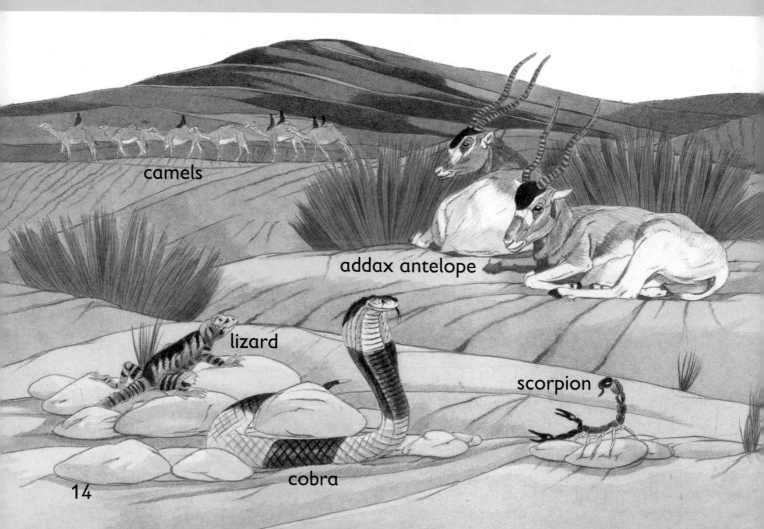

camels

addax antelope

lizard

scorpion

cobra

Fabulous Facts

Prickly plant

Desert plants called cacti have prickly spines to stop animals from eating them.

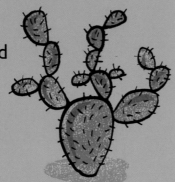

Sand mountains

Dunes are hills of sand that are made by the wind. The highest dune on Earth is the Cerro Blanco in Peru. It is around 1,176 metres high – more than three times taller than the Eiffel Tower in Paris, France.

Yakety yak

Ladakh, in India, is one of the coldest deserts in the world. Yaks who live there have thick shaggy coats to protect them from the freezing winds.

Desert wanderers

The Bedouin people of the Middle East and Africa are nomads. This means they move around the desert herding their animals.

Maaa!

Cool camels

Camels can drink a lot of water very quickly, then drink nothing for several days – very useful in dry deserts.

Wow!

The highest parts of the Sahara, in Africa, actually get snow in winter.

What are tropical grasslands?

Tropical grasslands are flat, open spaces covered with different grasses and a few trees. The African grasslands are home to some of the fastest animals on Earth, including cheetahs and gazelles.

elephants

cheetah

gazelles

giraffes

flap-necked chameleon

plain tiger butterfly

Fabulous Facts

Green giant

Tropical grasslands have a dry season and a wet season. There is very little rain in the dry season. In the wet season, some grasses can grow as tall as 2 metres – about as high as a door.

Water tree

Baobab trees have very fat trunks that they use to store huge amounts of water for the dry season.

Moving masses

Wildebeest migrate across enormous distances in Africa to find food and water. They live in large numbers to keep them safe from predators, such as lions.

I'm thirsty!

Wow!

The cheetah is the fastest land animal. It can run up to 100 kilometres an hour. That's almost as fast as the top speed a car can travel on a motorway!

Catch me if you can!

What is a mountain?

A mountain is a large area of land that rises high above the land around it. On the lower parts of a mountain, trees and other plants will grow. Only a few animals live in the cold and windy upper regions, where there is little soil for plants to survive.

golden eagle

ibex

mountain hares

Fabulous Facts

Top climbers

Ibex are a type of goat. They are brilliant climbers and live high up in the mountains.

Slowly does it

Mountain plants grow much slower than plants at lower levels. This is because they have to survive in very cold and windy weather.

Mountain fun

People often visit mountains on holidays and for sports, such as climbing, snowboarding and skiing.

Wait for me!

Ice rivers

Valley glaciers are huge, frozen rivers of ice that move very slowly down the side of a mountain.

Wow!

At 8,850 metres, Mount Everest, in Nepal, is the highest mountain in the world. It is about 60 million years old!

The poles

The Arctic and Antarctica are at the opposite ends of the Earth. The Arctic is in the north and Antarctica is in the south. Both are always covered in snow and ice, and are very cold all year round.

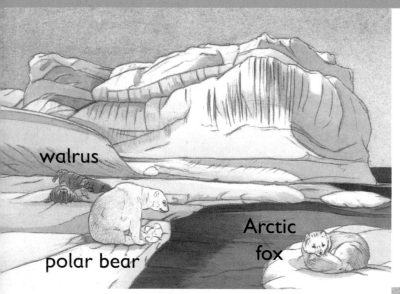

walrus

polar bear

Arctic fox

Frozen north

The Arctic is mostly made up of the frozen Arctic Ocean. Some southern areas are on land, where a few plants grow in the summer months. The centre of the Arctic is called the North Pole.

Antarctica

Antarctica is colder and windier than the Arctic. The land is mostly covered in frozen sheets of ice. The centre of Antarctica is called the South Pole.

albatross

Emperor penguin

humpback whale

20

Fabulous Facts

Funny birds

Penguins can look funny walking on land and they cannot fly, but they are very good swimmers.

Big bears

Polar bears have a thick layer of fat under their skin to keep them warm in the icy Arctic winds.

Hurry up, Mummy!

Ice explorer

Reaching the North and South poles is very hard. The dangerous conditions have meant that only a few have ever succeeded.

Hooray!

Day and night

During the Arctic summer, the Sun never sets and it is daylight all the time. In winter, the Sun never rises and it is always dark.

Wow!

Icebergs are huge floating chunks of ice. They are usually 100 to 500 metres wide, but some can be as big as a small country!

I'm just chilling out!

Oceans and seas

An ocean is a large area of salt water. There are five oceans on Earth and each one contains many smaller areas of water, called seas. Oceans and seas are home to fish and many other animals, such as octopuses, whales, sharks, turtles and crabs.

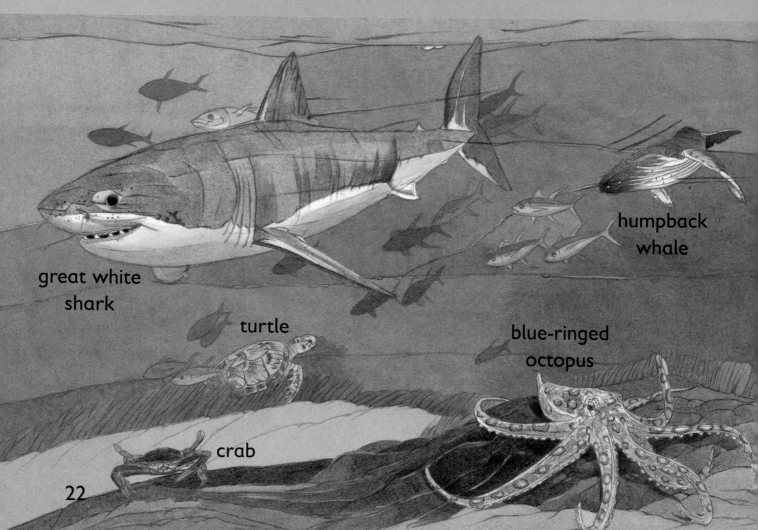

humpback whale

great white shark

turtle

blue-ringed octopus

crab

Fabulous Facts

Brilliant boats

We use boats to cross oceans and seas. Small fishing boats use nets to catch fish. Huge container ships carry everything from books to bananas from one side of the world to the other.

Underwater world

Coral reefs are made up of the skeletons of tiny animals called coral polyps. Many different sea creatures, from sharks and fish to octopuses, crabs and turtles live around coral reefs.

All afloat

The Dead Sea, in the Middle East, is very salty. The salt makes the water much 'thicker' than normal water, so it is really easy for people to float.

Look, I'm floating!

Wow!

Scientists go deep beneath the waves with special vehicles or robots that can explore underwater.

Who are you?

Where do people live?

People live all around the world. Lots of people live and work in cities. Others live in the countryside, growing crops and looking after animals on farms. A few people live in deserts, jungles and other places.

city

countryside

train

road

port

Fabulous Facts

Tribal clothing

The Inuit, who live in the freezing Arctic, wrap up with furs to keep warm. The Masai, who live in the Kalahari Desert in Africa, wear very little in order to keep cool!

World sport

Football is the world's most popular sport. Children only need friends and a ball and they can play anywhere!

Working families

In some parts of the world, the whole family works together to look after animals or grow crops for food.

Wow!

There are about 4 billion people in Asia — more than in any other continent. China, in Asia, is the country with the most people. Over 1 billion live there.

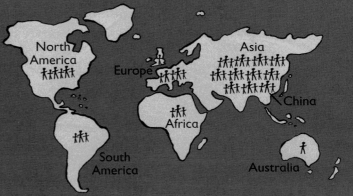

Help our world

We need to take care of the Earth now and in the future. Recycling glass bottles and other used things helps our world. It means we take less from the Earth to make new things.

How glass is recycled

1 People put glass in bottle banks.

2 The glass is collected and taken to the processing plant. Any metal or plastic tops are removed.

3 The glass is crushed into tiny pieces. These are taken to the glass factory.

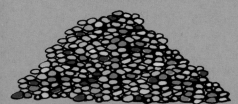

4 The pieces of glass are mixed with other materials. The mixture is then heated to a very high temperature until it melts.

5 The melted glass is poured into moulds to make new bottles and jars.

Fabulous Facts

Save energy

Replacing old types of lightbulbs in your house saves energy. New types of bulbs last about twelve times longer than the old ones.

Recycled paper

Paper is made from trees, but it can also be made from recycled paper. It takes only seven days for paper to be recycled and used to make new paper.

Save water

Turning off the tap while you brush your teeth saves about one bathtub of water each week.

Litter danger

Birds and other animals can be hurt or killed by litter. Make sure you recycle, or put rubbish in a bin.

Wow!

Some of our food is flown from the other side of the world. The aeroplanes cause pollution. To help reduce pollution, you can grow your own fruit and vegetables.

I love salad!

Record breakers

Biggest country

The biggest country in the world is Russia. It is over 17 million square kilometres. That's almost seventy times bigger than the United Kingdom!

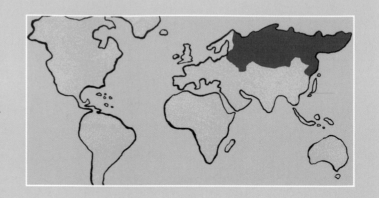

Biggest animal

The blue whale is the largest creature on Earth. It can grow to around 30 metres long – the length of three buses.

Tallest tree

The tallest tree on Earth is thought to be a coast redwood in California, USA. It is 115 metres tall. That's as high as a thirty-five storey skyscraper!

Coldest place

The coldest place where people live is Oymyakon in Russia. Temperatures can drop as low as −71°C. That's more than three times colder than inside your freezer!

Busy volcano

The volcano Kilauea, in Hawaii, has erupted forty five times in the last 100 years. It has been erupting almost non-stop since 1983.

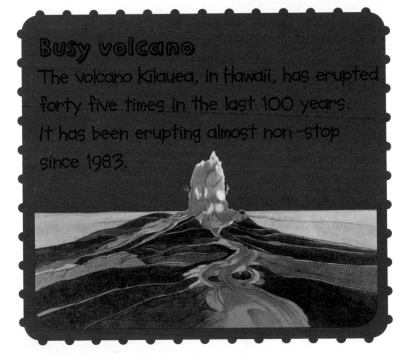

29

It's a funny world!

Why is the sea so friendly?

Because it always waves!

How do trees get on the internet?

They log on!

Which flowers are good at kissing?

Tu-lips!

What do clouds wear under their trousers?

Thunder-wear!

Where would you find an ocean without water?

On a map!

What did one volcano say to the other?

I lava you!

Glossary

energy   The ability to make things work.

flood   When water covers an area of land.

migrate   To move from one place to another at the same time each year. Some animals migrate to look for food.

orbit   The path of one object as it travels around another.

oxygen   The chemical that most life on Earth needs to survive.

pollution   A harmful substance in the Earth's environment that has come from rubbish or waste.

predator   An animal that hunts another animal for food.

recycle   To treat used materials or change them into new materials that can be used again.

solar system   All the planets and moons that go around the Sun. Earth is part of the solar system.

species   A group of animals or plants that are the same.

Sun   The enormous ball of gas that is at the centre of our solar system. The stars you see at night are other suns.

Index